Roth IRA

The Ultimate Guide to a Tax-Free Retirement

Table of Contents

tax-free, if they are qualified. To achieve this blissful state of a "qualified distribution", two conditions must be met - the Roth IRA must have existed for at least five years, and you must be 59 1/2 years old.

2.2. Growth and Tax Benefits with Roth IRAs

The Roth IRA grows over time with contributions and potential investment returns contributing to its growth. Ideally, the longer you let your account grow, the larger it becomes. An important feature is that any investment earning within a Roth IRA grows tax-free, safeguarding your nest egg from the IRS.

Tax benefits are major selling points of the Roth IRA. Here's the primary advantage - given that your contributions were already taxed, distributions in retirement are completely tax-free! This tax-free retirement income can be quite beneficial and can secure your retirement years, allowing you more economic freedom to enjoy the fruits of your lifetime's labor.

2.3. Converting Traditional IRAs to Roth IRAs

There's a methodology available to further widen your Roth IRA opportunities, particularly regarding the aforementioned income restrictions. Simply said, you can rollover or convert a Traditional IRA or another eligible retirement plan into a Roth IRA. Surprisingly, there are no income limitations on conversions, making this a practical route for high earners.

Note, however, that converted amounts (previously deducted) will count as taxable income during the year of the conversion. Make sure you prepare and budget for this potential tax liability.

2.4. Roth IRAs vs. Traditional IRAs

It's pivotal at this junction to differentiate Roth IRAs from Traditional IRAs. While both aim to foster retirement savings, they diverge significantly in their tax structures. Traditional IRAs offer tax-deductible contributions but levy taxes upon withdrawal, effectively reversing the Roth IRA's tax scheme. Confirming which IRA best suits you depends on a combination of factors, such as income level, retirement plans, and perceived future tax rates.

2.5. Taking Roth IRA Distributions

Plan properly, and your Roth IRA distributions offer a worry-free income stream during your retirement. However, premature or non-qualified distributions can be subject to taxes and penalties.

Generally, you can withdraw your contributions from a Roth IRA without taxes or penalties at any time. Earnings, however, face a 10% penalty if withdrawn before 59 1/2, unless certain exceptions apply.

In some cases, one can avoid the penalty (not the taxes), like first-time home purchases or specific medical expenses. A thorough examination of these exceptions would be beneficial before making any financial decisions of such magnitude.

2.6. Evaluating the Roth IRA

From potential high tax-free earnings to no required minimum distributions (RMDs), the Roth IRA is an attractive package for retirees. Flexibility exists, not just in your retirement income, but also in leaving a tax-free inheritance for your heirs.

But always remember the golden rule of investing: diversification. It's imprudent to rely solely on a Roth IRA for your retirement. Other retirement tools and accounts are available to ensure you have a diverse and robust financial portfolio to support your golden years.

This initial venture into the realm of Roth IRAs might seem a bit overwhelming, but as we dive deeper into the specifics, you will find the pieces of the puzzle fitting together. From contribution limits and tax rates to strategic investments and distributions, understanding the Roth IRA's basics is the key to unlocking the prosperous retirement you've always envisioned.

Chapter 3. The Magic of Compounding: Your Path to Growth

Let's dive in with enthusiasm into the wonderland of the compounding effect, an essential principle in finance that is the backbone of your Roth IRA. It's often said that those who understand interest earn it, and those who don't, pay it. This axiom holds when we consider the impact of compound interest in a Roth IRA, transforming it from simply an Individual Retirement Account to a potent growth engine.

3.1. The Promise of Compound Interest

Simply put, compound interest is earning interest on your interest. It is the reinvestment of your interest gains back into your IRA, resulting in the growth of your principal amount with each passing period. The effect is exponential, not linear, resulting in your wealth amassing at a faster clip as time passes.

Let's consider a hypothetical example. Let's say you open a Roth IRA with a contribution of $6,000 (the maximum contribution allowed due to age as of 2021), and the IRA earns a steady annual interest rate of 7%. With simple interest, in 30 years, you would have accumulated around $126,000. However, with compound interest, your Roth IRA swells to approximately $608,000 over the same period. More than four times the original amount!

How did that happen? The magic lies in the reinvestment of interest. Your $6,000 didn't just grow by 7% each year. Instead, each year's interest was added to the original amount to form a new principal, which then earned interest, and so on.

3.2. The Golden Rule of 72

The Rule of 72 is a simplified way to determine how long an investment will take to double, given a fixed annual rate of interest. By dividing 72 by the annual interest rate, investors can get a rough estimate of how many years it will take for the initial investment to duplicate itself.

Let's try it out with our earlier example. For an interest rate of 7%, the number of years it would take for your investment to double is roughly $72 \div 7 = 10.28$ years.

This rule isn't only a helpful tool but it also attests to the power of unleashing compound interest in your Roth IRA.

3.3. Key Drivers of Compounding: Time and Patience

Compounding is no overnight miracle; it requires two key ingredients: time and patience. Starting your Roth IRA at an early age gives your contributions the maximum possible time to grow. Thanks to compounding, individuals who contribute toward their Roth IRA from an early age can generate immense wealth over their working career.

Note that the power of compounding isn't just confined to your contributions, it extends to your earnings on those contributions. Since Roth IRAs have tax-free distributions, the exponential growth courtesy of compounding means a significant increase in your tax-free income in retirement.

3.4. Influence of Frequency on Compounding

Growth is quickened when interest is compounded more frequently. What does this mean exactly? Well, most investments compound interest annually, but some might do so biannually, quarterly, or even monthly.

Let's take an example where you invest $1,000 at a nominal interest rate (the stated rate of interest before accounting for compounding) of 5%. If interest is compounded annually, you'd have $1,050 after one year. If compounded semi-annually, your investment would grow to $1,050.94 and to $1,051.16 if compounded monthly. Over the short term, these differences may seem trivial. But the power of exponential growth over the long term can make this difference vast.

3.5. Sustained Commitment and Regular Contributions

Making regular contributions is an effective method to harness the power of compound interest. Let's say you start at age 25 and contribute $6,000 annually towards your Roth IRA with an average annual return of 7%. Compounded annually, by age 65, your Roth IRA would be worth close to $1.26 million, even though you only contributed $240,000 over the course of 40 years.

3.6. The Effect of Compounding on Diversification

Diversification is a risk management strategy where you invest in various assets in order to reduce exposure to any single asset. Over time, compounding significantly enhances the impact of diversification. As your diversified investments continue to yield positive returns, the returns too are reinvested into a diversified portfolio which further spreads the risk and enhances potential returns.

3.7. Conclusion: Compounding - The Silent Multiplier

Compounding, unlike market changes, is a feature within your control. Once you comprehend the full spectrum of its benefits, applying it isn't complex - start early, contribute regularly, and remain patient. With time, you will see your patience pays and your wealth grow. Keep in mind, compound interest doesn't discriminate; whether a seasoned investor or a beginner, the benefits are available to all who master its gradual, steadfast allure.

Remember, our financial goal, when planning for retirement, is not simply to save a certain amount of money. Rather, it's to amass a wealth furnace that's fed routinely and left to burn, unhindered, powered by the marvelous magic of compounding.

The key takeaway is that to amass substantial wealth in your golden years through your Roth IRA, you've got to let the compound interest work its magic. It starts with a commitment today, irrespective of how minuscule or grand. The marvel behind this simple concept is tangible within a Roth IRA, where your money grows tax-free as the years go by. This growth is only amplified by the fantastic magic that is compounding.

Chapter 4. Roth vs. Traditional IRAs: A Comparative Guide

In the realm of retirement strategies, the two most colossal titans undoubtedly are the Traditional IRA and the Roth IRA. Established in the annals of financial legislation to encourage wise, preemptive retirement planning, these tax-advantaged vehicles entice countless individuals each year. While they may seem similar, each holds an array of unique features and subtle differences. The key to unlocking the best retirement plan for your specific circumstances lies in deftly understanding these nuances.

4.1. The Traditional IRA Unveiled

An enticing, tempting path laid out for many is the Traditional IRA. Contributing to this type of account provides an upfront tax break – your contributions are tax-deductible. Consequently, the amount you contribute directly lowers your taxable income for that year, which can be an attractive proposition.

However, bear in mind this tax-deductibility hinges on your income level and participation in an employer-sponsored plan like a 401(k). As retirement inches closer and distributions begin, these will be taxed as regular income, a fact you would do well to remember.

Another telling feature of Traditional IRAs is the Required Minimum Distributions (RMDs). The age threshold for these is 72, post which the IRS mandates you start withdrawing a minimum amount from your account. Avoidance or deferral of these RMDs can result in hefty penalties.

4.2. Roth IRAs: A Deep Dive

Now, let's journey to the landscape of Roth IRAs. Introduced later than its traditional counterpart, a Roth IRA flips the tax equation around. You pay taxes upfront, meaning contributions are made with post-tax dollars. While the initial pinch might sting, the benefit lies in the complete tax-free withdrawals in retirement. That's right, every cent of growth your investments enjoyed, is yours to keep in their entirety.

There are no RMDs when it comes to Roth IRAs, unlike Traditional ones. You can let your investments grow potential wealth for as long as you live. Moreover, in the event of your demise, your heirs would inherit this account tax-free.

4.3. Income Limitations: Traditional vs. Roth

When marrying either IRA with your financial lifeplan, your income becomes a deciding factor. With a Traditional IRA, anyone with earned income can contribute, but not everyone can deduct those contributions on their taxes.

In contrast, Roth IRAs feature more stringent income restrictions. For single filers in 2021, for instance, the limit is a modified adjusted gross income (MAGI) of $140,000. The limit for married couples filing jointly is set at $208,000. Cross these thresholds and your eligibility to contribute to a Roth IRA diminishes.

4.4. Eligibility Past Retirement Age

While Traditional IRAs cease to accept contributions past the age of 70½ — effectively placing a time ticking counter on your investment, Roth IRAs lack such restrictions. The Roth continues to welcome additions as long as you live, provided you have earned income. This gives you more freedom and flexibility to manage your retirement savings.

4.5. Tax Diversification and Estate Planning

The last difference we will address involves a two-pronged approach: tax diversification and estate planning. Tax diversification is the concept of segmenting your retirement savings into different types of accounts to assist with unexpected tax situations in the future.

The Roth IRA shines here, allowing you to withdraw money in retirement without increasing your taxable income. This can be supremely beneficial when sudden expenses surface, or the regular income from a pension or Traditional IRA bumps you into a higher tax bracket. If you anticipate high taxes during your retirement years, a Roth IRA would be an apt choice.

Regarding estate planning, should you desire to pass a part of your retirement fund to your heirs, the Roth IRA proves advantageous. Your loved ones would receive the account minus any income taxes, a welcomed gift in times of grief.

4.6. The Verdict: Roth IRA Vs. Traditional IRA

The journey between Roth and Traditional IRAs is paved with gray patches rooted in personal circumstances and future forecasts. Whip out your financial map and evaluate key parameters relevant to you – current and future tax rates, income levels, contribution and withdrawal timelines, and estate planning goals.

A Traditional IRA appeals to individuals expecting to be in a lower tax bracket post-retirement and seeking a tax break now. A Roth IRA is more suited to those predicting high tax rates during their retirement years. These individuals are willing to pay taxes now for tax-free benefits later or plan to leave a tax-free inheritance.

But here's the twist. In the grand scheme of retirement planning, there's no edict stating you must pick one over the other. Harmonizing both to work in tandem can result in balanced, diverse retirement savings, delivering the boon of both worlds.

Remember, the goal is not to feel overwhelmed by the daunting task of making the perfect choice. Instead, focus on understanding your circumstances and assembling the components that best meet your needs. Pension, whether Traditional IRA or Roth IRA, ceases to pose a predicament when predilection meets prudent planning.

Chapter 5. Decoding the Eligibility Criteria for Roth IRAs

The foundation for creating your tax-free retirement via a Roth IRA is laid by first understanding the specific eligibility criteria. These regulations stipulate who can contribute to a Roth IRA and how much they're allowed to contribute. Our journey starts with decoding these guidelines, which will enable you to gain maximum mileage for your retirement funds.

5.1. Understanding Modified Adjusted Gross Income (MAGI)

To be eligible for a Roth IRA, the first thing to take into account is your Modified Adjusted Gross Income (MAGI). The Internal Revenue Service (IRS) deducts certain items from your Adjusted Gross Income (AGI) to calculate your MAGI. These items could be student loan interest, tuition fees, passive income or losses, among other things.

The ability to contribute to a Roth IRA is phased out over certain MAGI thresholds. There are different cutoff points for single taxpayers, married couples who file jointly, and married individuals filing separately.

For single taxpayers or heads of household in 2021: - The phase-out range begins at $125,000 MAGI. - The ability to contribute is completely phased out at $140,000 or more.

For married couples filing jointly in 2021: - The phase-out range starts from a MAGI of $198,000 - The ability to contribute is completely phased out at $208,000 or more.

For married individuals filing separately in 2021 (who lived with their spouse at any time during the year): - The phase-out range starts at $0. - The ability to contribute is completely phased out at a MAGI of $10,000 or more.

Be aware of your income range to ensure it falls within acceptable limits. It's crucial to calculate your MAGI correctly to avoid unnecessary penalties and headaches down the line.

5.2. Contribution Limits and Deadlines

Once you have confirmed your MAGI lies within the allowable range, your next step is to familiarize yourself with the contribution limits. The IRS specifies an upper cap on how much you can pay into your Roth IRA each year. These limits are dictated by your age.

The deadline to contribute to your Roth IRA isn't the end of the calendar year; instead, you have until the filing deadline (usually April 15 of the following year) to make your contributions for a particular tax year.

In 2021, if you were under 50, the maximum you could contribute to a Roth IRA was $6,000. For everyone 50 or older, 'catch-up' provisions came into play, allowing you to contribute an additional $1,000, giving a total limit of $7,000.

In addition to these general limits, the IRS notes 'contribution is reduced' if your MAGI falls within an applicable phase-out range (as outlined in the previous section). As your MAGI increases through that range, your allowed Roth contribution decreases, eventually reaching zero.

5.3. Prior Tax-Year Contributions

A notable advantage of Roth IRAs is the ability to make contributions to the previous tax year, even after it ended. This gives you a significant buffer period to add funds to your Roth IRA and claim the associated benefits.

You can contribute towards your Roth IRA as early as the first day of the fiscal year, and you have up until the individual tax return deadline (usually April 15), extending into the next year. Keep in mind, however, that any extensions applicable to your tax return filing do not apply to Roth IRA contributions.

If you haven't contributed the full allowed amount in the previous year and find yourself with some extra cash before tax returns get filed, you can include that as a prior tax year's contribution. This strategic move can help you maximize your Roth IRA contributions.

5.4. Distribution Rules

Understanding when and how you can take distributions from your Roth IRA is crucial to optimal retirement planning. Distributions from Roth IRAs can be classified as either 'qualified' or 'non-qualified,' each with its distinct tax implications.

Qualified distributions are tax- and penalty-free. To achieve this status, the Roth IRA owner must be older than 59.5 and meet the '5-year rule,' which dictates that the first contribution or conversion into any Roth IRA was at least five years ago.

Non-qualified distributions could potentially be subject to tax and/or early withdrawal penalties depending on the amount and the owner's age. It's vital to plan your distributions to maximize tax benefits and avoid penalties.

Understanding the eligibility criteria for Roth IRAs can significantly streamline your retirement planning process. By educating yourself on the intricate rules and guidelines, you arm yourself with the tools needed to secure a worry-free, tax-free retirement. Recognize your earning potential and make the most of it by adhering to the rules of the Roth IRA game. Your dream retirement lies within your reach, and it starts with understanding these basic eligibility tenets of Roth IRAs.

Chapter 6. Crunching the Numbers: Contribution Limits and Deadlines

When it comes to Roth IRAs, understanding the contribution limit is key to making the most of your tax-free retirement benefits. These limits govern how much you can pour into your account each year, and keeping up with them can offer you maximum long-term benefits. However, simply knowing the number isn't enough. Finding effective strategies to utilize the limit is equally important.

6.1. Understanding the Annual Contribution Limit

The annual contribution limit for Roth IRAs is defined by the Internal Revenue Service (IRS). It fluctuates each year depending on inflation and other economic factors. For 2021, the limit has been set at $6000 for individuals under the age of 50, and $7000 for those aged 50 and above. This extra amount, known as a "catch-up" contribution, is designed to help individuals who are nearing retirement age stow away additional funds.

Remember that these caps apply to your combined total contributions to both Roth and traditional IRAs within a single tax year. If you've already contributed $4000 to a Roth IRA and another $3000 to a traditional IRA in 2021, you hit the $7000 limit.

Contributions to a Roth IRA are made with after-tax dollars meaning you're funding the account with money that's already undergone withholding for income taxes. Conversely, Traditional IRA contributions are often tax-deductible, although there are certain eligibility rules for this.

Meeting the annual limit doesn't necessarily mean reaching it on the dot. You can contribute less, but do bear in mind that those contributions are your ticket to tax-free investment earnings, so any unused portion could be a missed opportunity.

6.2. Spouse IRA

Are you familiar with the Spousal IRA? If you're single-earning in your household, you can contribute to an IRA on behalf of your non-working or low earning spouse. Importantly, each of you can contribute up to the limit, essentially doubling your family contribution. These Spousal IRAs allow non-working spouses to build up their own retirement savings as long as their partners earn enough to cover the contributions.

6.3. Deadlines for Contributions

Contributions to your Roth IRA for a particular tax year aren't due on December 31. In fact, you have until the tax filing deadline (usually April 15) of the following year to make your contributions. This gives you an extra three and a half months to get your affairs in order and potentially make a last-minute contribution helping you max out your investment.

Fun fact: If the tax day falls on a weekend or a holiday, the deadline gets shifted to the next business day, which could give you even more time.

However, it's important to not rely on this safety net. Regular contributions throughout the year can put you ahead and help avoid a scramble for funds when the deadline looms.

6.4. Phase-out Range & Income Limits

While Roth IRAs are astoundingly advantageous, they aren't accessible to everyone. If your income exceeds a certain threshold, your ability to contribute gets reduced - the upper-income limit - and gradually leads to a complete phase-out. The phase-out range and income limits are contingent on your filing status and are updated annually. You'll need to consult the IRS's most recent guidelines for the latest figures.

When your income falls within these phase-out ranges, the maximum you can contribute to your Roth IRA gradually decreases. If your income exceeds this range, you become ineligible to contribute for that tax year.

6.5. Consequences of Excess Contributions

Take caution not to exceed the contribution limit, whether due to an oversight or misunderstanding. Excess contributions are subject to a 6% excise tax. This tax applies each year the excess remains in your account.

Furthermore, if you withdraw excess contributions before filing your tax return or October 15 (whichever comes first), you can avoid the 6% excise tax. To withdraw excess contributions, ensure to also remove any earnings generated by the overages. If you don't, they may be subject to both taxes and penalties.

IRA contributions may seem like a numeric jungle. However, understanding the underlying principles, restrictions, and strategies can usher in a pot of gold at retirement. So go, unravel the numeric knots, leverage the limit and secure a resplendent, tax-free finale to your professional journey! Remember, we are here to assist you in decoding and mastering IRAs. Let's march together toward a worry-free, tax-free retirement!

Chapter 7. The Art of Conversion: From Traditional IRAs to Roth

In the realm of retirement planning, one of the vital maneuvers often overlooked is the conversion from a Traditional IRA to a Roth IRA. This strategy can pave the way for a less-tax-burdened retirement, providing an unexpected windfall during your golden years.

7.1. Why Convert Your Traditional IRA to a Roth?

The foremost reason for a Roth conversion is the profound benefits of tax-free withdrawals. Traditional IRAs offer tax deductions on contributions but impose taxes on distributions, while Roth IRAs operate in reverse. With a Roth IRA, you pay taxes upfront on the money you contribute or convert, allowing you to benefit from tax-free distributions in retirement.

Another catalyst for converting your traditional IRA is to evade the required minimum distributions (RMDs), which mandate you to take minimum withdrawals from your account starting at age 72. Roth IRAs do not have any such withdrawal obligations during the owner's lifetime, granting you more control over your retirement funds.

7.2. The Tax Implications of Converting

While a Roth conversion can provide a wealth of benefits, it's essential to understand the tax implications. The amount converted is considered taxable income and is thus taxed at your regular income tax rate. This means you'll have to foot a tax bill in the year you make the conversion. However, experts often advise high-earning taxpayers to convert during low-income years to minimize the tax hit. It's best to consult with a tax professional before committing to a conversion.

[NOTE]
The conversion may bump you into a higher tax bracket; hence, spreading the conversion over multiple years is often advised.

7.3. Deciding When To Convert

Timing is key when contemplating switching to a Roth IRA. It's prudent to convert when your current taxable income is low or when you believe your tax rate will be higher in retirement than it is now. This is typically during your early or late career stages - switching during high-earning years isn't as beneficial due to the higher tax implications.

7.4. The Conversion Process

If you've decided that you would benefit from a Roth conversion, the next step is to understand the conversion process.

1. Open a Roth IRA account if you do not already have one.

2. Reach out to the financial institution where your Traditional IRA is held and request a Roth conversion.

3. Decide how much you'd like to convert and pay the taxes due.

The financial institution will guide you through the process, ensuring you successfully convert your Traditional IRA to a Roth IRA.

7.5. The Five-Year Rule

The "five-year rule" for Roth conversions stipulates that you must wait five years or until age 59½, whichever comes first, before withdrawing the converted funds tax- and penalty-free. The clock starts ticking from January 1st of the year of your conversion. If you withdraw before satisfying this condition, you may face a 10% early withdrawal penalty.

7.6. Reconversion and Recharacterization

A reconversion occurs when you convert your Traditional IRA to a Roth, then convert it back to a traditional IRA, and convert once again to a Roth. You might opt for a reconversion if the value of your converted assets sadly decreases due to market fluctuations, and you want to avoid paying high taxes.

Recharacterization, on the other hand, is reversing your IRA conversion as if it never happened. You have until the due date of your tax return, including extensions, to recharacterize your Roth conversion.

7.7. The Bottom Line

The decision to convert from a Traditional IRA to a Roth is entirely personal, heavily reliant on your current financial status, future income predictions, and overall retirement strategy. While tax-free income in retirement and the absence of RMDs are tempting, it's essential to weigh these benefits against the immediate tax payment. As always, it's advisable to consult with a tax professional or financial advisor to help navigate this complex decision.

Now that you're armed with all the necessary knowledge about the art of Roth conversion, take that step closer to a tax-free, worry-free retirement. Think smart, plan strategically, and ensure your golden years are indeed golden!

Chapter 8. Harvesting Tax Benefits: Roth IRA Distributions

Understanding the fundamentals of Roth IRAs distributions and how they can yield powerful tax advantages, is a crucial pillar of strategic retirement planning. With clever application, you can fully optimize these benefits, resulting in a tranquil, stress-free retirement.

8.1. Knowing The Basics

The magic of Roth IRA rests in the promise of tax-free distributions. A primary difference between a Roth IRA and a traditional IRA is when you pay taxes. With a traditional IRA, you contribute pre-tax dollars, and the withdrawals are taxed. However, in a Roth IRA, you contribute post-tax dollars, meaning your distributions, inclusive of contributions and earnings, will be entirely tax-free provided certain conditions are met.

8.2. Meeting The Conditions

These tax-free benefits are subject to the following two conditions popularly known as the '5-year rule' and 'age rule,' respectively:

1. *5-year rule*: You must have owned your Roth IRA for at least five tax years before taking tax-free distribution on the earnings.
2. *Age Rule*: You must be at least 59 and a half years old at the time of the distributions.

Following these rules will help avoid penalties when claiming your tax-free benefits.

8.3. Understanding Qualified Distributions

Distributions that meet the 5-year rule and age criteria are termed as 'Qualified Distributions'. A distribution is deemed qualified and hence penalty-free if it meets both of these conditions. Your contribution to the Roth IRA is always available for withdrawal tax and penalty-free. The qualifying rule applies only to the earnings part of the distributions.

8.4. Understanding the 5-Year Rule

The 5-year rule creates a waiting period intended to deter short-term usage of a Roth IRA. This period begins on January 1 of the tax year you made your first contribution to the Roth IRA. Also, contribution rollovers from other retirement accounts can have their own five-year period.

8.5. The Age Rule

While 59 and a half might seem like an arbitrary age, it's a common threshold for retirement accounts. Early withdrawals before 59 and a half, excluding certain exceptions, are subject to penalties. However, after turning 59 and a half and passing the 5-year ownership test, you can withdraw your Roth IRA distributions tax and penalty-free.

8.6. A Closer Look at Early Distributions

While Roth IRA encourages you to wait till the qualifying period or age, circumstances might make you consider an early withdrawal. If you've not reached 59 and a half years or have not met the 5-year rule, pulling the money out could attract taxes and penalties. However, there are exceptions:

1. First-time home purchase: Up to $10,000 may be exempted from penalties.

2. Disability: If you become disabled, withdrawals might be exempted.

3. Higher education expenses: Can be exempted from penalties under certain conditions.

4. Medical expenses: If these exceed a certain percentage of your income or are for health insurance while unemployed, you might be exempted.

5. Inheritance: Beneficiaries of a Roth IRA might be able to withdraw tax and penalty-free.

8.7. Interaction with Other Retirement Accounts

Rollovers and conversions from traditional IRAs or 401(k)s into a Roth IRA introduce another level of complexity.

One key thing to remember is that each conversion or rollover has its 5-year period. This 5-year rule begins on January 1 of the year of the conversion, regardless of when the conversion occurred within that year.

For example, if you transfer money from a traditional IRA to a Roth IRA in December 2022, the clock starts on January 1, 2022. Therefore, the money becomes eligible for withdrawal on January 1, 2027.

8.8. Planning for Succession

As a part of your estate planning, considering the Roth IRA's inheritance rules is essential. When a spouse inherits a Roth IRA, they can treat it as their own IRA or as an inherited IRA. Non-spouse beneficiaries, on the other hand, must withdraw all funds within ten years of the original owner's death. In both situations, these distributions are usually tax-free, provided the original owner met the 5-year rule.

8.9. Leveraging Tax-Free Growth

Time is a significant factor in maximizing your Roth IRA benefits. The more years you allow your investments to grow, the more potential they have to compound, increasing the tax-free portion. The ability to leave your money untouched until you need it, combined with the tax-free growth potentiality, makes Roth IRA a robust tool for enjoying a secure, worry-free retirement.

Leveraging a Roth IRA distribution's power lies in understanding the rules and strategically planning your contributions and withdrawals. As a part of your retirement plan, it can effectively aid in shaping a successful and serene sunset phase.

Chapter 9. Mature Strategy: Roth IRA for Seniors

Understanding the function and benefits of a Roth IRA can make a massive difference in your retirement experience. As a senior preparing for or currently navigating retirement, it is crucial to be armed with knowledge, shed light on the convolutions of tax laws, and take control of your future. Let's embark on a journey to learn about the advantages of Roth IRAs for seniors, conversion strategies, withdrawal rules, and estate planning merit.

9.1. Benefits of Roth IRA for Seniors

Roth IRAs are considered a significant tool for seniors due to their unique benefits. Unlike Traditional IRAs, Roth IRA contributions are taxed upfront, allowing for tax-free withdrawals in retirement. Here's why it's outstanding:

- Retirement Income Control: Having a Roth IRA allows you to manage your retirement income and consequently your tax bracket better. Withdrawals from a Roth IRA are not considered taxable income, giving you greater control.

- No RMDs: Unlike Traditional IRAs, Roth IRAs do not require Required Minimum Distributions (RMDs) during your lifetime. This means you can leave your funds to grow tax-free indefinitely if you do not need them.

- Tax-Free Legacy Planning: Roth IRAs are also advantageous from an inheritance standpoint. As long as the account has been open for at least five years, your beneficiaries can also enjoy tax-free withdrawals.

9.2. Roth Conversion As A Strategy

Some seniors may possess a Traditional IRA or a 401(k) and are considering switching it to a Roth IRA. Before diving in, know that there are potential tax implications. Any pre-tax contributions and earnings moved to a Roth IRA will be taxable in the year of conversion. However, the benefit of tax-free withdrawals in the future may outweigh this one-time tax hit.

Consider your current tax bracket, expected future tax bracket, time horizon, and ability to pay the conversion taxes with non-retirement funds when pondering over conversion. Some may find it useful to spread out conversions over multiple years - a strategy called "Roth Laddering".

9.3. Roth IRA Withdrawal Rules

If you're right at retirement age, you might be wondering how the withdrawal rules work. In a Roth IRA, your original contributions can be withdrawn anytime tax-free, as already taxed at the time of contribution. However, the rules differ for withdrawing earnings.

In order for earnings to be withdrawn tax and penalty-free, the Roth IRA account must have been open for at least five years and one of the following conditions must be met:

- You are aged 59 ½ or older
- The funds are used to purchase a first house (up to $10,000 lifetime limit)
- The withdrawal is due to death or disability

9.4. Estate Planning with Roth IRAs

One of the valuable features of the Roth IRA is its utility in estate planning. Leftover Roth IRA funds can be passed to heirs tax-free, which can be a substantial benefit. The account can continue to grow as the beneficiary can stretch the tax-free withdrawals over their life expectancy.

Note that The Setting Every Community Up for Retirement Enhancement (SECURE) Act of 2019 modified the rules for inherited IRAs. Most non-spouse beneficiaries are now required to deplete inherited accounts within 10 years, but the funds remain untaxed.

9.5. Conclusion

In the world of retirement planning, Roth IRAs offer unique hope in creating a tax-free retirement life for seniors. The gift of tax-free income during retirement, no RMDs, and potential benefits for legacy planning make these accounts an attractive retirement strategy. As with all things finance, remember that everyone's situation is unique. Always consult with a tax or financial advisor to understand how a Roth IRA or a conversion to a Roth IRA aligns with your personal circumstances.

Embrace the retirement years with the confidence of a well-optimized strategy, understanding the inner workings of your tools, and securing your and your loved ones future. Because retirement should be about enjoyment, not worrying about taxes.

Chapter 10. Avoiding Pitfalls: Common Errors and How to Dodge Them

From the get-go, it's imperative to understand that while Roth IRAs hold great potential to embellish your retirement years with financial security, they also come with a few key aspects that have potential pitfalls. So, let's journey forth and uncover these common obstacles, arming ourselves with the knowledge to evade them.

10.1. Familiarizing Yourself with Roth IRA Rules and Limitations

If you cross the income thresholds set by the Internal Revenue Service (IRS), you won't be allowed to contribute to a Roth IRA. These thresholds change every year, so it's critical to stay current. Direct contributions to a Roth IRA are not tax deductible, unlike a traditional IRA. However, qualified withdrawals are tax-free. However, if you withdraw earnings before age 59 1/2 and before having the account for five years, you will typically owe income tax and a penalty.

10.2. Exceeding Contribution Limits

Contributing beyond the limit set by the IRS is one of the most frequently encountered errors among Roth IRA holders. In 2021, the limit for contributions is $6,000, or $7,000 if you're aged 50 or older. Overstepping these limits can lead to penalties and a complicated tax scenario in the future. Thus, be mindful of these boundaries and ensure you are accurately tracking your contributions.

10.3. Early Withdrawals

Withdrawing your earnings early from a Roth IRA can cost you indeed! The IRS defines 'early' as any withdrawal before you turn 59½ years old. Unless certain exceptions apply, these early withdrawals may be subject to income tax as well as a 10% penalty.

10.4. Non-Qualified Withdrawals

Even after the age of 59 ½, your withdrawal might not be completely tax and penalty-free unless it's a qualified distribution. It's a easy mistake to make, but the implications can be severe. Remember, a withdrawal can be classified as 'qualified' only if it satisfies two conditions — it is made after five years since the opening year of the Roth IRA and the distributor is aged 59½ years or above.

10.5. Miscalculating Five-Year Rule for Withdrawals

Don't let the 'five-year rule' trip you up. It mandates that a Roth IRA be open for at least five tax years before qualified distributions can be made. This rule often leads to confusion and miscalculation. Be aware that this countdown begins from the first tax year you contribute to your Roth, not from the date of setting up the IRA.

10.6. Mistimed Conversions

Converting traditional IRA or 401(k) funds to a Roth IRA can offer several benefits. However, mishandling the conversion due to mistimed action may lead to unnecessary taxes. To make the most of the conversion, it would be best to convert when your income and tax rate are lower and to ensure you have money outside your IRA to pay the taxes due for the conversion.

10.7. Not Understanding Required Minimum Distributions (RMDs) Rules

Roth IRAs are not subject to RMDs while the account owner is alive, unlike other retirement accounts. This often leads to confusion and misunderstanding. Understanding the RMD rules thoroughly can help maximize the benefits of your Roth IRA.

10.8. Forgetting Beneficiary Designations or Not Keeping Them Current

Another seemingly small error that may lead to major complications in the future, is assuming you've named the correct beneficiary. Or forgetting to update the designated beneficiary on the Roth IRA when life circumstances change.

To effectively dodge these common IRA pitfalls, it's crucial to keep abreast of changing IRS rules, monitor your contributions and distributions, understand the implications of conversions, and routinely update beneficiary information. With a careful, informed approach, you can be assured of cruising seamlessly through your journey to a tax-free, worry-free retirement!

Chapter 11. Case Studies: Real-life Applications of Roth IRAs

Roth Individual Retirement Accounts (IRAs) have emerged as substantial tools when planning for retirement. They offer potential tax-free growth, with the added advantage of tax-free withdrawals during retirement. They are particularly beneficial if you expect your tax rate to be higher during retirement. Now, let's delve into some real-life applications and case studies to better understand the practical implications of a Roth IRA.

11.1. The Potential of a Roth IRA: The Case of Jenny

Jenny, a 25-year-old recent graduate, is all set to join her dream job at a tech start-up. Even though her initial salary isn't high, her earning potential is considerable. Understanding the advantage of starting early, Jenny decides to contribute the maximum amount permitted to a Roth IRA every year. Let's assume an average 6% annual return. Jenny continues this annual contribution of $6,000 for 40 years until she retires at 65.

Calculations reveal that her total contribution would amount to $240,000. However, the power of compound interest in this tax-free environment translates her contribution to just above $1,000,000. At retirement, Jenny can withdraw from her Roth IRA tax-free, granting her a million-dollar tax-free retirement fund.

11.2. The Power of Conversion: The Case of John

John, a 45-year-old successful business owner, has been diligently contributing to his Traditional IRA over the years. His business is flourishing, and he is situated in a high tax bracket. John learns about the possibility of converting his traditional IRA to a Roth IRA. John decides to perform a conversion.

There are tax implications, as he has to pay the tax bill on the conversion. However, he calculates the potential for tax-free growth and withdrawal after his retirement and decides it is beneficial in the long run.

Keep in mind that IRA conversions require strategic planning. Timing and taxation are critical factors impacting the success of a conversion.

11.3. Inheritance Planning: The Case of Emily

Emily, a 70-year-old widow, has accumulated wealth over her life, including a substantial Roth IRA. She wants to ensure her heirs benefit from her assets. Roth IRAs have an extraordinary feature – unlike traditional IRAs, they aren't subject to Required Minimum Distributions (RMDs) during the owner's lifetime.

Emily does not have to withdraw any funds during her life, allowing the Roth IRA to keep growing tax-free. After Emily's death, her children inherit the Roth IRA. They must take distributions, but the "stretch" provision allows them to take these distributions over their life expectancy, keeping most of the fund in the account growing tax-free.

Again, estate planning with Roth IRAs requires careful tax and legal considerations, but the benefits can be highly rewarding especially for high-net-worth estates.

11.4. The Flexibility Game: The Case of Robert and Linda

Robert and Linda, 35 and 33 respectively, are a young married couple. They have been contributing the maximum allowed limit to their Roth IRAs. An unprecedented medical emergency occurs, leaving them with substantial medical bills.

One advantage of a Roth IRA is that contribution withdrawals are tax and penalty-free at any time for any reason, providing more flexibility than traditional IRAs. They decide to withdraw the principal amounts they contributed to their Roth IRAs, providing them immediate relief while leaving the earnings untouched to keep growing tax-free.

Roth IRAs offer a greater degree of flexibility for unexpected emergencies or even other financial goals due to their unique withdrawal rules compared to traditional IRAs.

The above real-life applications showcase the utility, flexibility and strategic benefits of Roth IRAs under a variety of conditions. Retirement planning is not a one-size-fits-all science, but with sound financial decision-making and strategic planning, including the astute use of tools like Roth IRAs, you can optimize your financial future and navigate your way to a worry-free, tax-free retirement. Remember, the journey to successful retirement requires a map – and a willingness to embark on the journey. Let your journey be enlightened, empowered and enthused with the power of knowledge.